MW01100587

SIMPLY MADEAR
'It Ain't My Business, But'. . .

by BEATRICE WATSON, R.A.

A story of maternal love, courage, wisdom
and humor compiled and written with
narration and poetry

FOREWORD BY DR. MARGARET T. G. BURROUGHS

Printed in Victoria, Canada

Cover design and layout by Andrea Green
Book cover and graphic design concepts by Beatrice Watson
Book cover and interior illustrations by Jamar Rahasean Arthur
Book typsetting, layout and design concept by Angeli M. Olive-Stalling
Edited by Sandy Hillard and Carol Sawall-Smith

Photos from personal library of author.

All graphics relating to any subject matter throughout this book are fictional and any
likeness to anyone living or dead is unintentional and coincidental.

National Library of Canada Cataloguing in Publication

Watson, Beatrice
 Simply, madear : it ain't my business, but-- / Beatrice Watson.
ISBN 1-55369-612-3
 1. African-American women--Poetry. 2. Inspiration--Poetry.
 I. Title.
PS3623.A87S55 2002   818'.609   C2002-902516-8

Direct all inquiries to the author at:

JA-WA PRODUCTIONS LTD.
P.O. Box 438941
Chicago, IL 60643
Fax# 773-667-0068

TRAFFORD

This book was published *on-demand* in cooperation with Trafford Publishing.
On-demand publishing is a unique process and service of making a book available for retail
sale to the public taking advantage of on-demand manufacturing and Internet marketing.
On-demand publishing includes promotions, retail sales, manufacturing, order fulfilment,
accounting and collecting royalties on behalf of the author.

Suite 6E, 2333 Government St., Victoria, B.C. V8T 4P4, CANADA

Phone	250-383-6864	Toll-free	1-888-232-4444 (Canada & US)
Fax	250-383-6804	E-mail	sales@trafford.com
Web site	www.trafford.com	TRAFFORD PUBLISHING IS A DIVISION OF TRAFFORD HOLDINGS LTD.	
Trafford Catalogue #02-0425		www.trafford.com/robots/02-0425.html	

10   9   8   7   6

SIMPLY, MADEAR
'It Ain't My Business, But…

≈ ≈

≈ ≈

ACKNOWLEDGEMENTS

This small treasure of stories, quotes, and poems, is a tribute to my mother Azella, who gave us memories to live by and to my father Joe, the anchor that remained steadfast!

I personally dedicate this work to my siblings and their families: Joe Jr., Hazel their children; Gregory, Julian, and Renee, Sharon (Charlene), Charnet, Tommy, Velma their children; Tiffany, Kevin, Teresa and Kim; Sandra, her children; Wesley, LaDale and Rusan; James, Diane, their children Christal, Monique, Kelly and Leah; Deborah, her husband Albert and daughter Tracie. To Rodney, Gary, his wife Mary, their daughter, April and to Denise and her husband Bernard, their children, Anictra, Lamar and Denard. Also, to my daughter Mia, her husband, J. Paul, their children J.P., Joel and Joshua. And to all of my parent's great-grandchildren, etc. May the strength and wisdom of both Madear and Daddy serve as your inheritance of endless wealth.

To my extended family and friends, you know who you are. To Bob, a special friend.

Special thanks to Angeli M. Olive-Stalling of **Desktop Perfect,** Andrea Green of **Creative Designing**, and my sister Deborah Reyes; industrious women who worked diligently and patiently to achieve the correct formatting and layout of manuscript and cover design.

To all the readers, may you find pleasure in these precious selections, and whenever needed, may it also serve you like a beacon in the fog.

Beatrice Watson

PREFACE

This book is written in loving memory of the countless mothers across the globe that forged the way for many women of today. They were the mothers who stood up against all odds and raised their children with love, dignity and respect for others and themselves. They dealt with life and problems with the limited resources and knowledge they had at the time. If we could combine their wisdom, with the knowledge that we have acquired, in helping to solve family and personal issues in our lives and affairs, it may prove to be of great advantage. Somehow decades of their natural, maternal gift for parenting was tossed aside as being too restrictive and unrefined. This was replaced with modern 'How to Books' on raising children and molding families.

Being a parent, and during my years of working with youth groups and social service organizations, I've noticed the changes in the attitude of our youth today. As a sales specialist, conducting business with young mothers, I observe how they deal with their toddlers and adolescent children. They would yell, curse, pull and almost plead with them to behave as they attempt to conduct business in a nervous and stressful state.

This book certainly is not a quick fix for parenting problems, but based on the turmoil, and unrest of our families and youth today, a dose of innate wisdom from the past can't do us any harm. It might even make a difference.

It is for the young and the old. The calming
voice in the night from a gentle yet firm
woman, many of us refer to as Mother, Mom, or
'Simply Madear'.

A heartfelt collection of serious, sometimes
emotional and humorous quotes and paraphrases,
that depict old, southern values of child
rearing and family unity. It focuses on
Azella a woman called 'Madear' by her ten
children and other young people as well (who
was married for over fifty years). It takes
you on a journey through the exciting era of
the 50's through the 70's in Detroit Michigan,
culminating during the turbulence of the late
90's.

FOREWORD

Each generation has a story to tell and wisdom to impart to its youth. Even though each person must test the waters and stumble as they grope for the answers to their own existence, there are already tried and proven parts to the puzzle born out of toil and sweat.

Through this unique book 'Simply Madear', Beatrice Watson has charted her experiences and growth as a child in Detroit, under the loving guidance of her mother Azella, and her father Joe. Together they raised a family of ten children with simple means and strong values, a bond lasting close to sixty years.

Beatrice, the second eldest, shares words of wisdom by and in the voice of her mother, Madear, that are full of courage, warmth and humor. This excellent saga is greatly enhanced with narration and thought provoking poetry by Beatrice.

'Simply Madear' does not only bring enjoyable reading, but will certainly dismiss the myth that the majority of African-American families are dysfunctional. It should be received warmly by individuals of all ages and walks of life.

For those of you who can remember, you will re-visit a magical time of community and family pride; for others, you will be able to experience laughter, joy and a time of uplifting inspiration.

Dr. Margaret T. G. Burroughs
Artist, Author, Co-Founder, Emeritus
Director of the DuSable Museum of African American History Chicago

Tammie,

May God bless
and keep you in
His grace.

[signature]

Black Words of Wisdom

Next to God we are indebted to women, first for life itself, and then for making it worth living.

Mary McLeod Bethune

("Famous Black Quotations," Janet Cheatham Bell)

♦

We need to uncover and (Re)write our own multistoried history, and talk to one another as we are doing so.

Gloria T. Hull

("The Black Woman's Gumbo YA-YA" Terri L. Jewell; Quotations by Black Women)

♦

It was there, in the Detroit Brewster Project that I met Mary Wilson and Florence Ballard. She and Florence went to Northeastern High while I went to Cass Tech. The three of us hit it off. Of all I do, I am most proud of my children. I teach them to respect others and to treat all people fairly. It hasn't always been easy balancing the many roles and demands of being a working mother and wife, but the rewards are golden.

Diana Ross

(Memoirs "Secrets of a Sparrow") Headline Book Publishing, 1994

INTRODUCTION

WE WERE A FORTUNATE GROUP OF BLACK CHILDREN, RAISED DURING THE LATE FORTIES THROUGH THE SIXTIES IN A LOW TO MODERATE INCOME ENVIRONMENT, (FIVE GIRLS AND FIVE BOYS). WE WERE FORTUNATE IN THAT WE EXPERIENCED THE JOYS AND FULFILLMENT OF BOTH PARENTS.

ONE OF THE MAIN BENEFITS AS WELL, WAS THE FACT THAT OUR MOTHER, WHOM WE AFFECTIONATELY CALLED 'MADEAR,' WAS A LOVING, WISE AND STRONG-WILLED WOMAN. SHE HELD OUR FAMILY TOGETHER THROUGH ALL ITS UPS AND DOWNS, GUARDING AND NURTURING, AS WOULD A LIONESS OVER HER CUBS. HER SIMPLE, SOUTHERN, TRADITIONAL VALUES AND WISDOM GUIDED US THROUGH MANY TIMES OF FEAR AND SADNESS, AS WELL AS HAPPINESS AND JOY. SHE, LIKE SO MANY MOTHERS OF THAT ERA, GAVE US WORDS OF ADVICE, WHETHER WELCOMED OR IMPOSED, THAT MORE TIMES THAN WE LIKE TO ADMIT, WAS PROFOUNDLY ACCURATE AND TIMELESS. HER HUMOR WOULD CHARM YOU, HER ANGER COULD SHAKE YOU, AND HER UNCONDITIONAL LOVE WOULD ALWAYS AMAZE YOU! I RECALL HER TEACHINGS AND THE MANY WORDS OF GUIDANCE THROUGHOUT MY CHILDHOOD.

AS AN ADULT, THOUGH A DISTANCE AWAY, WE KEPT IN CONSTANT COMMUNICATION. WE SHARED MANY MOMENTS OF MOTHER/DAUGHTER CONVERSATIONS ABOUT MATTERS THAT CONCERNED US BOTH. SHE POSSESSED A JOLLY NATURE AND QUICK WIT THAT SEEMED TO SHARPEN WITH AGE.

OUR MOTHER PASSED IN LATE FALL OF 1993 AT 72 YEARS OF AGE, LEAVING A GAPING VOID IN ALL WHO KNEW AND LOVED HER. IT INSPIRED ME TO SHARE WITH OTHERS THE LEGACY OF THE LOVE, WISDOM AND COURAGE WHICH EMBRACED US THROUGH HER YEARS AS A PARENT AND MENTOR.

BEATRICE WATSON

Part One and Two
The Early Years/Molding a Family

Tells of a young family, Madear and Daddy, migrating from the south to the north with their children in search of a better life, including the simplicity of raising children during the late forties through the seventies. **(Poems)** "As I Reflect" and " Childhood Friday"

Part Three
Adolescence and Sex

The coming of age during the late fifties in Detroit, Michigan. The anxiety of a mother dealing with the growing pains of adolescent teens with the basic maternal instinct of right and wrong. She guided and directed their growth and development through church and the community.

Part Four
Religion
Tells of the strong southern religious beliefs and folklore that Madear, and other parents of her era used to instill morality and righteous behavior in the shaping of the family unit during the fifties through the seventies. **(Poems)** "To You My Child" and "God and I".

Part Five
When a Child Leaves Home
Breaking away from the family nest. Children of adult age finding their way, armed with the basic training received from their childhood **(Poem)** "Farewell My Nest"

Part Six
Loss of a Child
The coping of parents in confronting the death of their child, as they keep their inner strength and faith. **(Poem)** "Friend or Foe"

Part Seven and Eight
Love and Marriage/It Ain't My Business, But. . ..

A mother's input on her adult children in making sound decisions with their head and not just with their heart. The inability of a mother to release her adult children to their own fate. (**Poem**) "Love's Quiet Moment"

Part Nine and Ten
Taking Responsibility/Pride and Self Confidence

Now a grandmother, Madear talks on crime and violence as she passes her wisdom onto the third generation. She teaches them to take responsibility for their own actions and take charge of their lives.

Part Eleven
Aging and Fear
The deep emotions of aging parents and the fear it generates.
(**Poem**) "As Time Moves On"

Part Twelve
Violence and Crime
It talks about the changes in our youth and society as safety in the streets and our homes are threatened.
(**Poem**) "Baby Boy"

Part Thirteen
Illness and Death of a Parent

The agony of watching the debilitating effects of illness and coming to grips with the death of a parent. "This woman who had been with me my whole life, long before I knew who I was, was about to leave me". (**Poem**) "Here We Stand"

The story ends with a poem that stands alone, but sums it all up, giving us courage to look ahead.
(**Poem**) "Mother"

Madear and Daddy

IN THE BEGINNING...

Azella Watson
(MaDear)
18 Years Old

Joe Watson
Around 24 years old

~ ~

Your Daddy worked in the mines with my Poppa in New Castle, Alabama. One day Poppa brought him home to have dinner, hoping to match him up with one of his six daughters. He was tryin to marry off the older ones first(smile). But your Daddy took to me. His mother was half Indian and his Daddy was just a plain mean, old, Negro cuss. Your Daddy and his brother Mose thought they was some hot stuff; high yellow, runnin 'round flirtin with all the girls. I showed him I was a proud one, I wasn't gonna be so easy to catch, no matter what my Poppa said! When we finally got together, one of his two sisters ran home, told their mother that he had taken up with a real black gal. For a long time I tried kissin up to his family. One day I said, 'To hell with that, they have to take me the way I am.' I was smarter than any of them and your Daddy loved me, that's all that counted. I got along with them just fine after that.

THE EARLY YEARS

8

The weeds grew tall, almost above our heads, as we forged our way toward the hill where we could look down at the train as it passed. Tommy was a toddler holding tight to my hand. I was only a year older. We tugged closely behind my brother Joe Jr., who was the oldest by one year. Lead by an older cousin of about ten, we watched excitedly as the midday train rushed by, sending out a loud howling sound. It carried people we could hardly see to strange places we knew nothing about, and left a trail of dust as it sped away. Ever since a letter had arrived telling us that our Madear, (given name Azella) would be coming soon to take us up north, where she and Daddy had gone ahead, and where Daddy had found work in an auto factory, we asked a thousand questions of our Granny.

All Granny would say was that, 'Your momma will be here soon by train.' So we kids just hoped that one of the trains would stop any day now and our Madear would get off.

Much of those times are hazy in my mind, but the train ride back north still stands out vividly. She looked strange to us at first, it had been some months since we had seen Madear, according to my Granny. Tommy hardly remembered her, so he clung to me for awhile.

We played cheerfully up and down the aisle of the train. Joe Jr. toyed around with us for awhile, then pushed us aside when he grew tired. We would run back and forth occasionally to a brown paper bag our Granny had packed, full of fried chicken, biscuits, fruit and slices of delicious butter poundcake that only she could bake. We would eat and ask so many questions about up north and about our Daddy (given name Joe), whom Granny always referred to as 'Manchild'. It was such a strange name to us that when she used to say, 'I am going to tell Manchild on you if you don't behave', we would straighten up right away.

Madear wore some kind of cologne that smelled of fresh rose petals or jasmine. Her upper arms were plump and soft. As the evening grew late, she held Tommy against her bosom, as Joe Jr. and I snuggled our heads against each of her upper arms, safe and warm.

MOLDING A FAMILY

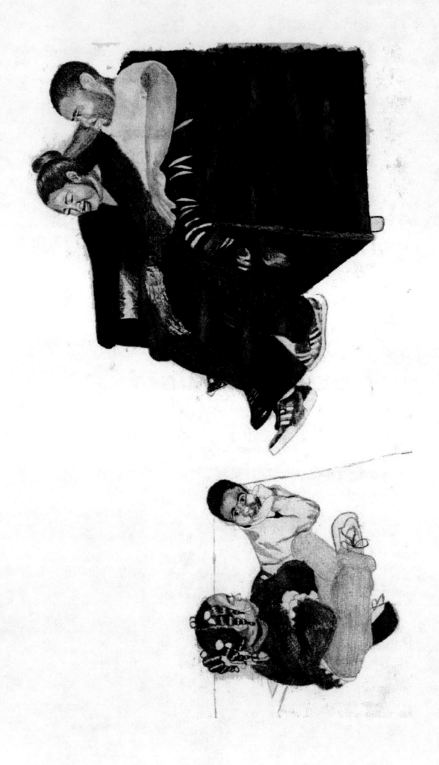

The hot summer months kept everyone up late into the night, sitting around on their porches. Our parents talked with neighbors across their yards, with the playful sound of children and their games echoing in the air. The sky was so clear you could see the Big Dipper and other clusters of stars dancing in the heavens. In the mornings a rainbow would flaunt its colorful rays across the sky, after a warm summer rain, leaving the earth gleaming with the fresh, clean smell of the soil. A simple time, a simple place, branded in my mind forever.

"As I Reflect"

As a child I walked briskly down long sunny paths, hand in hand with others who played openly and gaily, never worrying about tomorrow or the many whys that filled my little thoughts.

It was a time when the earth burst with the fragrance of new blankets of grass and the sweet smell of morning rain that tapped on my window pane. Daffodils, and dandelions and other flowers closed their petals to rest when the evening came.

Now, as I reflect on precious moments far away in my past, many things have changed, including the way I was. But as I look around me, nostalgia fills my heart, for then there was still the freshness and the beauty that sparkled through each strand of new spun grass.

~~

Now you sit in this room 'till you learn how to behave. You runnin 'round tellin all the kids on the block there ain't no Santa Claus. Spoilin their Christmas 'cause you didn't get what you wanted. You be thankful for what you got. There some fruit in your box, candy, a colorin book, and a pretty 'lil doll. So what, 'cause she ain't white and don't have much hair like the dolls in the Sears catalog. She look just like you, brown and pretty, so ain't nothin wrong with that doll! Ain't nothin wrong with you neither, but stubborn!

We were always so excited during the Christmas season, because of all the fun we'd have shopping with Daddy for our Christmas tree; a project in itself. It had to be just right, Daddy always picked the same kind of tree, full and tall, with a long stem at the top, so that we could easily place a star there. Each of us kids would try to outdo the other, creating paper decorations in school for our tree. We'd drink eggnog and stay up late a few days before Christmas decorating the tree. Then finally Christmas Eve arrived; the house smelled of pine with the aroma of cakes and pies baking in the oven. Madear would bake a cake for each of us with the icing or topping of our choice. Mine was always chocolate with pecans. Helping out in the kitchen, I enjoyed mixing the frosting and then, with my finger, licking the bowl clean afterwards. Cutting onions and washing dishes were my most dreaded chores. Later I'd go and sit quietly looking through a Sears catalog at a beautiful ivory skinned doll with long flowing hair; every girl on the block pretty much wanted one. I put in a request to Santa and placed it under a slice of cake and a glass of milk, left to refresh him on his journey. The little black, hard/rubber dolls I would see while shopping with Madear or Daddy had lines painted on their head, indicating hair, or they had short, nappy hair that you could do nothing with.

Finally, the house was quiet and all of us kids tossed nervously in bed. One particular Christmas I decided I would confront Santa and make sure he understood what I wanted, so I slipped into the broom closet. Cramped but determined, I stayed there dozing off and on, for what seemed like hours. My heart began beating rapidly when finally I heard the boxes rattling and voices whispering. I slowly and quietly crept out of the closet only to see Madear and Daddy removing items from beneath their bed and from the clothes closet. As a child, that was the most disappointing sight of my life. But looking back now I only have warm and happy feelings about it, because of the love our parents showed for us and the sacrifices they had to make to bring holiday joy to us in the best way they could. Time has since proven those to be the most memorable Christmases I've ever had.

~ ~

When grown folks talkin you children go from underfoot and go somewhere and play. Ain't nothin we talkin 'bout your business!

~ ~

While your Daddy and me go take care some important business, we want you to look after each other. You all old enough to behave yourselves and I better find this house the same way I'm leavin it!

I used to often wonder what grown-ups meant by business; I figured it must have been something special. Whenever Madear and her friends would get together in the living room laughing and talking or when she was on the phone, we were always instructed to go and play somewhere else in the house, but I would always find an old Reader's Digest or a pad of paper and sit quietly in a corner, reading or writing something, within hearing range, as they talked about domestic life or the latest gossip on the neighborhood grapevine. Now Daddy was different, he didn't seem to care. Whenever he had an occasional visitor or was cutting someone's hair, (something he learned to do naturally and made extra pocket change from), we played all over the place while they talked about sports, the workplace or the job the President was doing, from their viewpoint. A lot of information my Daddy got on sports as well as politics came from Madear, since she was an avid sports fan and often read to Daddy out loud from the newspaper, since his reading was limited. The rest he got first from radio, later from television. Madear would take advantage of those occasions when Daddy was at home with customers or building or repairing something around the house, by taking a break from us all. She would visit a neighbor or her old cousin Rosie, who lived up the street. Her cousin's house was crammed with old musty newspapers, with furniture and knic-knacs everywhere. Everytime we went to the store we had to go by her house to find out if she needed something. She would reward us with some old, sticky, hard candy that probably had been sitting around since that past Christmas. There was this huge old picture of her when she was younger, that was hanging on her wall, with eyes that seemed to follow you all over the room. I remember when she died, of all things Madear got that picture and hung it on our wall. One day Tommy threw a rubber ball and knocked the picture down, breaking the glass and the wooden frame around it. We were all relieved about it but Madear was furious, mainly because we weren't supposed to play ball in the house. Daddy teasingly commented that cousin Rosie would wake from the dead about her picture. In addition to being punished, Tommy was real scared about that. A little while after, when Daddy and Madear had to go out for a short time, I, being the most creative and curious of the bunch, (I always had some antics up my sleeve) decided to have a trial for Tommy for breaking cousin Rosie's picture. Tommy went on trial and Joe Jr. spoke in his behalf, I spoke for cousin Rosie, Sandra and James

22

(Bumpty), who were just toddlers, were the jury. With all the lights out I dramatized and conjured up a scary scene that frightened all of them to pieces, especially the guilty and sensitive one, Tommy, who, until this day is probably still afraid to sleep in the dark.

~ ~

Go put on your sweaters you two, and get your
red wagon so you can go with your Daddy to
the Eastern Market to shop. You don't mind
eatin, so you better not mind helpin!

Going shopping with Daddy at the Huge Eastern Market was like an endless parade; all types of people sampling, tasting and purchasing fresh produce from farmers who would come together once a week from all around Michigan. Madear hardly ever went, it was always Daddy and two of us kids; one pulling the red wagon and the other following behind, making sure everything stayed on securely, while Daddy stacked items in it. I remember the long mile walk to the market and then the tedious walk through the vast mile-long shopping arena. Summer or winter the juicy sweet fragrance of red delicious apples and plump oranges or raw peanuts made up for the foul scent of live poultry and the putrid smell of fresh slaughtered meat that hung heavy in the air. Holiday time at the market was always fun, people moved slower, smiling at each other, and giving greetings. We always ended up at Daddy's favorite pub, where we'd rest before journeying home. Daddy would have a mug of ale and we were treated to either a hot dog or the most delicious, heartiest bowl of chili that I've ever tasted.

~ ~

How would you kids like another sister or
brother? Don't you be frownin either!

The family was growing rapidly. Madear was pregnant every year and Joe, Tommy and I were in charge of the dirty diaper detail. A messy, dreaded chore for all of us, having to dunk the waste, rinse out the diaper and hang it up to dry, awaiting wash day, which was done on your hands and with a scrubboard, for it was years before we could afford the convenience of a washing machine. I remember at one point during those times I staged a non-speaking boycott against my Daddy and Madear, with the support of Joe and Tommy, to halt them from having more babies, which resulted in spankings for all of us. An effort that was lost anyway since they ended up with a total of ten children. I often reflect on how my parents managed to deal with and get through the adventuresome mishaps and childhood pranks I had a hand in. Today I'm thankful that my mom and dad disregarded our protest and gave us the benefit of a large, close-knit, loving family. Aside from the problems that most siblings have, I have found my sisters and brothers to be of great comfort and joy.

One of those non-speaking times was during a family photo session. Madear had gained weight and was pregnant with Sharon and didn't want to go, but Daddy insisted. Joe

Jr., Tommy and I decided not to cooperate, so we made funny faces as often as we could during the shooting. It didn't matter because Daddy bought all the pictures anyway.

(Annual family picture)
Standing, left to right, Madear,
Tommy, Joe Jr., Daddy, Me, (Beatrice),
Sitting; Sandra and James (Bumpty)

~ ~

We didn't plan to have so many children. It just happened. They didn't have all the things they got now to control it, but it worked out alright, 'cause your Daddy is a good provider and a hard worker. Don't have no fancy things, but we get by. Me, the mother of ten children. My, my!

~ ~

I never knew my mother, she died when I was just a small child. Not like your Daddy, he had both his parents, and they had over twelve children. I never knew what it was like to have a mother. I'm proud that God blessed me so that I could feel and give the love I never had. One day you kids will know how important that is.

~ ~

You kids have no excuses for not makin somethin of yourselves, you have more chances than your Daddy and me. Your Daddy wasn't even allowed to go to school after age seven, he had to go work in the fields. I went as far as the tenth grade, then up and got married. Ain't no reason why you all can't go as far as you want to!

~ ~

You all ain't gonna grow up fighting each other like your father and his folks... My sisters and me, we were raised to love each other, you family, not heathens. I don't ever want you to raise your hands to hit the other as long as the days you live.

As our family grew, so did the hard times. I am sure there were many for my parents, with factory cutbacks and all, but we never knew a hungry day. That's not to say that we didn't have to eat a lot of dishes such as beans and cornbread more often than I'd like to remember. But it filled our stomachs and made us appreciate the days when we had a variety of food on our plate.

Our Daddy bought fruit by the bushel for eating and canning. Many evenings we would sit and watch Madear cooking apples. Lots and lots of them. The house was full with the smell of ginger and cinnamon as she seasoned large pails to be preserved and finally filling glass jars, leaving them to cool overnight on the table. The sweet aroma would fill the entire house and we knew the next days we would be feasting on hot, delicious apple cobbler, fried pies and fruit jam.
Having so many children, Daddy would buy everything in bulk, such as giant boxes of cold cereal, corn flakes and others. We would thrill from eating out of large containers. For a few days after pay day there was always plenty   of   treats.

"A Childhood Friday"

Fridays had always been full of happy anticipation, Madear was especially cheerful, singing about the place, because there would be no heavy meal prepared that day, dad would receive his weekly pay.

Us kids would play outside, close around the house, for our old pop would be coming home soon, with his green lunch pail, across the large vacant lot.

There would be some sweets tucked away in a brown bag and a special treat, gotten from a deli not far away from Dad's bus stop up the street.

I would always save my nickels, my brothers would quickly spend theirs. Oh, I remember Fridays and enjoyed them so with glee, but our father, shoulders drooping, always seemed so tired, as he drank slowly from his large beer mug and occasionally sighed.

His life was like a ritual, from one day to the next, the same empty lunch bucket, as like a broken soldier, he walked across the dirt filled lot. Yes, I remember Fridays, the fun, but now mostly I remember the rest my father never got.

It was always so good coming home from school, running in past the screen door, where Madear was always waiting, greeting us with hugs and hushing us up so that she could hear the final episodes of her soap operas before finishing dinner. There was no rushing back outside, our chores awaited us.

The evenings brought family conversation and laughter. Those were precious times, whether we were sitting around the kitchen table doing homework, or playing games on the floor, there was always Daddy and Madear there with us, disciplining, guiding, supporting and lovingly caring for us. As children, there were no bad times, only memorable ones.

Daddy never took a day off, except for holidays and forced vacations, on those times Daddy would work around the house, mending. He would sometimes go rabbit hunting with his best friend, with dogs he had ordered from a catalogue. Hunting reminded him of his childhood, and of his life in the south. I remember Daddy building us a swing in the backyard, that was connected to the house and a big oak tree. Many hours I would swing, day dream and write.

~ ~

My sisters, my brother and me used to hate
this old, mean woman my Poppa took up with
one time, 'cause he needed someone to help
raise us. She would beat us all the time when
he wasn't there, for barely nothing at all.
She made dresses for us out of old burlap
sacks and kept money our father gave her for
us. One day a black cat took up at our house
and used to snare up at her every time she
would hit one of us. It jumped up and
scratched her arm real bad one time, so she
took it away and we never saw it again. We
always thought it was our mother who'd come
back through that cat. Not long after that
Poppa got rid of that woman. Now there some
some good step-mothers, better than some
mothers, but I pray to God to be 'round to
raise my own children.

~~

You kids is blessed, we one of the first to get a television on our block. Now you can invite some of your friends over to look at it, and Bea I better not hear 'bout you chargin anybody anything either!

~ ~

It's hot, leave the door cracked for air tonight, make sure the screen is shut tight so that them nasty flies won't get in!

ADOLESCENCE AND SEX

41

The curiosity of our youth filled us with excitement and thoughts of careless adventure. The natural changes in my brothers' voices, from boyish wailing to a husky roar, was astonishing. Tommy, who I used to hold down in wrestling matches as he called out to Madear for rescue, overnight became a giant who could hold me at bay with almost one hand.

Now, I shyly wore a training bra that adorned my blossoming bosom, soon after, there was Vaseline greased legs, small waist, tight sweaters and hooped ballerina skirts. Joe Jr. had girls tagging behind him on a regular basis as he played the role of hard to get and unconcerned. While our lives soared through adolescence, Madear's tone changed from that of cuddling and nurturing to caution and apprehension.

~ ~

No matter what, I will always love you children, and if you ever do wrong, I will stand by you through it all, but, don't ask me to lie for you!

~ ~

If you can stay out of the mirror long enough, 'Miss Ann,' you can finish your housework. Whatever you look like will be there tomorrow, but I intend for this ironin to be done today!

~ ~

Boy, you gonna get somethin over the head if you keep slippin out at night, and coming back late through the window. Ain't nothin out there at night but trouble.

~~

Just 'cause you on your monthly now, don't
mean you no grown woman round here. Your body
just done gone ahead of your mind, that's
all!

~ ~

You is a big girl now, so show respect for
your father and brothers. You wear more than
just a slip when you walkin 'round the house.

~~

No phone calls comin in or goin out of this
house after seven o'clock on school nights,
and you gals better not let me hear you
runnin no boys down on this phone like no
hussy, anytime!

~~

If you carry yourself like a young lady, chances is, you will be treated like one!

~~

Why can't your baby sister go with you,
whatcha gonna be doin she can't see?

~ ~

Don't ask me how, but I am your mother and
I'll know if you're lyin or not!

~ ~

Keep your legs closed, your dress down, and
don't be huggin up with no boys in cars or
anywhere else, or you might get somethin more
than what you lookin for!

~ ~

You know that gal up the street went and got her a baby don't you? Well, she done just added a whole lot of problems on to her young life. It's hard enough to raise kids with two parents. She gonna find out that it ain't no doll she carrin 'round.

~~

Just cause you made one mistake don't mean you gotta wallow in it. You hold your head high and with God's help you can make a difference in your life from here on in.

~ ~

You boys better listen to your Daddy about messin with girls, 'cause if any gets in trouble, and says it's yours, then who's to say it ain't; so you keep your pants zipped up or you gonna be responsible for whatever happens!

Many of my friends, like me had brothers whom
we often snickered with as small children as
we observed each others private parts. We
knew the difference between the male and
female body, even though our mothers never
came right out and said the word penis, we
figured that was the forbidden object they
were warning us against. During those times
there were no laws in place for 'Date Rape'
though I am sure it occurred more often than
girls talked about. Isolated cases of incest
or child molestation were also things that
you would hear about through fragments of
low-toned conversations from the adults. I
once overheard Madear talking to one of her
shattered sisters in the south who had
discovered that her young daughter had been
molested over a period of years by her
stepfather, and had gotten pregnant as a
result. Everyone was furious but nothing was
done about it. He left town and was never
heard from again. In general on dates most
boys, after getting aroused during an erotic
session of kissing and fondling, with fingers
everywhere, would stop short of penetration
when girls said no! Most girls paid the
price for not listening to their mothers,
because there were times many girls had to
claw their way out of heated situations,
after taking petting to it's limit. It was a

time when the preservation of virginity and the 'good girl' image was extremely important. I do believe that our era saw the last of the so-called 'Good Girl's Club'. The female virtue, the precious gift of self, for far too many, was no longer held in high regard.

Looking back, it seemed that information was given to us in fragmented pieces, like clues to a complicated puzzle. Parents expressed what they felt the best that they knew how at the time. Even though limited in detail their messages were full of wisdom, teaching us the basics in love, respect and honor. It behooves us to take lessons from our past and continue to add the missing pieces to a quilt that has been in the making by mothers for centuries.

~~

You boys gonna learn to clean and cook just like the girls. You ain't guaranteed to have somebody take care of you the rest of your life.

When Madear wanted to put the fear of the Lord in you, she would tell one of her many yarns...

~~

Your Daddy said his Mama told them there was once this girl whose father had died, and after he did she got so wild her Mama couldn't do nothin with her. She stayed out all night, and all the boys snickered about her. One night she was comin home real late and had to pass the old graveyard where her father was buried. Pretty soon everyone for miles round could hear her screamin, and cryin out, 'I am sorry Poppa, please don't hit me no more Poppa'. They say when they saw her runnin out of the darkness her clothes was hangin torn round her, and her arms had big red welts on them. After that no-one ever saw her outside after dark again. And years after she died herself, people said they could still hear her sometimes late at night screamin and cryin from that old graveyard. I don't know how true that is, women in the south used to tell a lot of strange stories, but I never made light of them.

~ ~

You be home on time, 'cause you don't want me to come to that party to get you, you really will be doin some dancin then!

~ ~

It's alright if you want to be a big screen star, you can be whatever you want to be if you work at it. Your Daddy says that only thing Negro women can be in the movies is maids. But all that will change one day, but even if it don't, you would only be playin like a maid, but you would be livin like a star!

We never thought too much about racism, other than what we'd hear Madear and Daddy talk about, and the Emmett Till killing in the south. Our high school, Northeastern, had a few white kids, they kept to themselves as did the light-skinned children; no-one seemed to care or put up a fuss. The whites would come into our neighborhood as bill collectors, workmen, or policemen. There was this one restaurant near the shopping district, it was beautiful like something from a lost era, and the neighborhood had just changed around it I guess. The name of it was the Roma Cafe; my girlfriends and I would sometimes stand near watching the big cars and see the high-fashioned white people going in and coming out. We'd attempt to peer through the thick block glass front, only to see outlines of figures and catching a glimpse of the white table clothes, the shining crystal, and the tailored waiters, whenever the door would open.

After a while the doorman would run us off. I'd tell Madear that one day I would drive up in front of a beautiful place like that and be escorted in. She smiled and said sure, but until then keep from around there.

We grew up in a time when there was music and singing on almost every street corner, crooners looking for that big opportunity, Motown beginning. It was commonplace for my brother Joe and Smokey Robinson and others to sit around on our porch harmonizing or just rapping. A female group, later known as the Supremes, would often sing in the variety show at Northeastern high, where I belonged to a theater club. I was so serious with it that I would often wear my costume to my other classes in an attempt to develop my character. Martha Reeves, (later of the Vandellas), and I would walk to school many times, along with my best friends Lawanna, Tess, and Evon, talking about our dreams and aspirations. My brother Joe did back up singing on a hit recording 'The Entertainer', under the guidance of a man we called 'Pops'. Pops brought together talented young people at a field house, in the Brewster Projects, where Diana Ross and Florence Ballard lived with dreams of stardom.

My brother's career however was short-lived after getting married. I played it safe and dealt with community theater and writing in an attempt to appease my creative urge.

My father had always been the one to take us shopping at the beginning of the school year. Like a goose with its' ducklings we'd follow him downtown to Sam's Cut Rate store. There we would get the basics, penny loafers or black and white oxfords, plain cotton dresses for the girls, shirts and jeans for the boys. I often longed for the clothes from the fancy stores where some of the other girls shopped. Joe Jr. Eventually began buying his own clothes from resale shops with money he'd earn doing odd jobs. He dressed in slacks and fancy shirts throughout high school. Tommy never made a fuss about it one way or the other.

When graduation time came around daddy refused to buy the different dresses suggested for the variety of ceremonies. But it all worked out, Aunt Annabelle bought my prom dress and Madear found money by budgeting real tight. Somehow she always came through.

~ ~

Don't fret 'bout what your Daddy say baby,
you gonna get a new dress for your class
luncheon. I'll look at the house money, and
I'll find a way!

~ ~

A person is judged by their underwear, in case anyone ever has to see them, so keep them and yourself clean, you never know what might happen!

~ ~

Your brother Joe is bringin a girl home to dinner tonight, I want all of you to act like you got some sense, and I hope your Daddy will eat at the kitchen table tonight, instead of in front of the television.

~ ~

Now, you keep this in your pocket gal, you
never go nowhere with nobody, without some
money, you don't know what might happen and
you want to get out of some place in a hurry!

~ ~

That boy, Joe Jr. always teasin Hazel, sayin they kept him up so late at his bachelor party, that he don't remember ever sayin 'I do', at his weddin the next day 'cause he blacked out just before. But, she says he did and the minister signed the paper, so that's all that counts!

~ ~

You all got a nephew, and I got my first
grandchild. My firstborn got him a boy, ain't
that something!

RELIGION AND FAITH

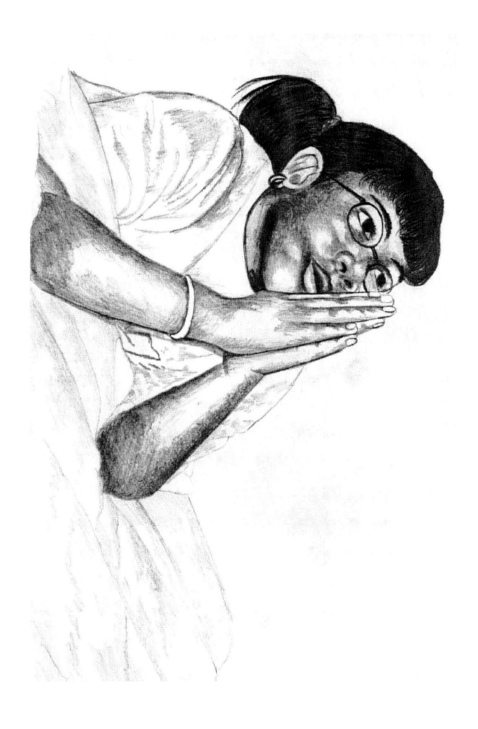

~~

God is good. He let me see you all get grown.
Many nights I prayed hard for all my babies,
and I give thanks for you, 'cause you God's
babies first, 'fore you mine!

~ ~

God gave you everythin you need to do good. He owes you nothin, but you do owe yourself and Him to do the best you can with your life!

~ ~

If you go to church just for show, then you
might as well go gallivantin' for all the
good it's servin' your soul, or the Lord.

~ ~

Save a nickel out of what your Daddy gave you today for church Sunday, you always give somethin back to the Lord to show your thanks.

~ ~

Without faith you just standin in the middle
of nowhere, not knowin' which way to go.

Church on Sunday was an all day event. I had two aunts that along with my mother made a great impact on my religious upbringing. Aunt Mattie, my father's sister was a spiritualist and her church was a small store front with a high fan blowing hot air in the summer months. All the women wore white uniform dresses and the men wore dark suits. The intoxicating music of piano and tambourines rang out into the street. Members would feel the Holy Ghost and with beads of perspiration crinkling their neat dresses and starched shirts they danced as in a trance and spoke in a strange tongue. It was truly something to see.

My mother's sister aunt Annabelle, was a member of a holiness church that took me through my adolescent years. It was also a full day of activities and services. Women dressed in tailored fashions with large sculptured hats. Paper fans in hand waving in pursuit of a cool breeze, which only added to the discomforts coming from the heated kitchen, where a Sunday fundraising dinner was prepared weekly. The aroma of buttered dinner rolls, lemon pound cakes and juicy fruit pies hung heavy in the air. It caused great distraction as children moved about restlessly in their seats in anxious anticipation.

The first acknowledgment of my writing ability came from one of their annual talent competition where I won first prize for an original poem entitled 'God and I'.

Churches served as the foundation that helped to build the character of young people, and aided them in identifying their creative talents. Choirs were a springboard for greats like, Sam Cook, Gladys Knight, Aretha Franklin and many others that brought rejoicing and inspiration through their jubilant   sounds.

"God and I"
(The faith of a child)

God and I, we do things together everyday.
He is with me wherever I go, in school or at play.

God and I walk together on dark and lonely streets
no fears, no doubts and no strangers do we meet.

If kids laugh or poke fun, about some silly little thing,
I would smile to myself and at peace I would be,
because no matter what goes down, it's only God I see.

Sometimes there are things that try to make me feel down,
but I don't worry because God is always around.

Sun up, we welcome a bright new day, chasing butterflies,
enjoying the sweet smell of a rose as we fan away a
buzzing
bee.
Then quietly, with my diary, God and I would rest beneath
a willow tree.

He is my best friend, my Father and my Mother too.
He watches over all there is, protecting and guiding me
and you.

At night the moon shines bright and shadows dance across
my room.
Unafraid I close my eyes and drift off peacefully to sleep.
I am all wrapped up in Gods' loving arms, I know my
safety he will keep.

Written at age 15

"To You My Child"
(A mother's prayer)

God is with you, not just today when all is shiny and bright, but when this moment is no more than a pin point in the corridors of your mind.

God's love surrounds you not just this moment when spirits are high and worries are small, but when your friend's face beside you is as hazy as a figure far away in a fog.

God smiles on you, not just right now when eyes are clear and the world is bright, but when hope begins to falter and problems seem to mount.

God stands by you, not just on occasions when laughter fills your heart and happiness spills over, but when loneliness creeps in and the doubt weighs heavily on your back.

God brings you comfort, not only in instances when youth is your friend and flowers blossom where you walk, but when limbs get weak, when spring seems cold and years get too short.

God walks with you, not just when a loved one takes you by the hand and leads you safely every step, but when you look at the world through your own eyes, to see what must be done, and against all odds you take your proper place in the sun.

To you my child, as you follow your chosen path. The rewards will be so great, if you take God along as your constant mate.

Written for my daughter Mia's 16th birthday

WHEN A CHILD LEAVES HOME

"I'll never leave you Mom!", proclaims a sleepy-eyed, curled up six year old, after a bed-time story and a prayer has been said and a good-night kiss is given. The mother smiles warmly and knowingly, tucking the covers around the bed. All too soon the child grows up and does leave, and, the mother soon passes on. A moment in time is gone, but the maternal love and the lessons learned as a child, forever goes on.

My brother Joe Jr. had gotten married to his high school sweetheart, become a father, and now had gone off to the service. Tommy was making plans on going to the army, and I was helping Madear around the house with my younger brothers and sisters. I was working part-time and whenever I could I'd take part in a local drama group, where I grew more intensely interested in theater after being introduced to it during high school. There was no money for college, but I longed to see life. I was eager to get away, like my brothers, to take life on, to find my way.

~ ~

I've been savin up a little money to put with
what you've got. Rose and Grace is in
Chicago, you can stay with them, they say
it's okay. Lots of jobs there, better than
here in Detroit. Maybe you can get in
college, you got a lot of dreams in your head
and some of them will come true. You been a
big help with the kids, but it's your turn.
Remember what I told you. It's all up to you
now!

~~

We raised you all the best we knew how, now
go out there and show the world what your
best is.

~ ~

Once you know who you are, then everything
else is clear.

~ ~

No matter if you married or not, always have you some money of your own put away. You won't have to beg nobody for nothin!

"Farewell My Nest"

Farewell my nest, for the moment had arrived, the smoke from the train spread through the terminal. The entire family had come to see me off. A couple of my smaller sisters tugged at my dress to get my attention. Two of my younger brothers played cheerfully around the station.

I smiled as the tears rolled down my face, partly out of sadness and a little out of fear. I suddenly understood how my older brother felt when he left for the service a year ago, now my moment had arrived.

'Now remember to write often, you hear?' informed my mother. I knew I would miss it all, the laughter, the family struggles and their joys. Most young girls leave their fathers home to wed, but I chose the world, so the moment had arrived.

'All aboard', announced the conductor, as my parents kissed me softly upon the cheek. More tears and hugs, then finally the waving from the platform grew dimmer and dimmer as I pressed my face against the train's window pane, I knew then my life had taken a new turn. The moment had arrived. Farewell my nest, for I know I will never return home as a child again!

LOSS OF A CHILD

~~

Hello baby...Your brother is gone, he's gone, oh Lord, my child is dead! (Phone drops, there is crying and screaming).

Marriage, the army, and three small children later, the eldest, our brother Joe Jr. was gone forever. It sent a bolt through our close knit family, testing our foundation!

~ ~

I knew somethin was wrong, when your brother
came by the house early that mornin, on his
way to the factory two blocks down. That was
strange, 'cause he would always come by at
lunch time. He talked for awhile, sayin he
had just bought this 'bad suit' and he wanted
your baby sister to keep the kids for him and
Hazel on New Year's Eve. Then he smiled
through his teeth, like he always did, and
looked at me for a long time, then said, 'Bye
Madear', and he left walkin, leavin his car,
somethin he never did, 'cause he truly loved
it. He never made it to lunchtime. Round
eleven-thirty, some white men came to my
door; somehow I knew he was gone before they
had a chance to tell me, the machine that had
killed another worker a month earlier, had
taken my son's life.

(cont.)

For a long time that car wouldn't start no
matter what, 'til I went out there and just
said, 'Let it go baby, you can't take it with
you, let it go'. Then I started it right up.
He was buried in that suit he talked about
that day.

~~

Whether we like it or not, you can't take a thing with you, but you sure can leave good things to be remembered by!

~ ~

He was my firstborn...Shortly after his
death, I hurt so bad, I asked myself, if
there was any of my children I could have
sacrificed for his life if I had a choice,
who would it be? I couldn't think of not a
one I could give up, not a one, includin him.
I love you all just the same!

A few years later...

~ ~

I know you gonna be shocked when you see your sister. Remember she always wore a size fourteen; well, she's ninety some pounds now. The doctor say she got somethin called lupus. I just pray they can do somethin bout it!

"Friend or Foe"

Life goes on, or so they say.
You learn to direct your steps
in other ways.

Death. . .
The cold, dark visitor that
every now and then drops in..
There are times he is regarded
as a friend to the sick, the
aged and some lost soul
But then again. . .
Is he a foe that enters through
some uninvited door, to pull a
baby from its mothers arms, to rob
a young maiden of her lovers charms?

Friend or foe, the message comes
loud and clear,
that old man death, who lags
somewhere close behind, can
cheat you of your dreams and
steal you swiftly away from
Father Time!

Sharon's funeral was on a cool misty day. Her long illness had finally taken its toll. Even though we expected it, the sadness was still overwhelming, and Madear's loss of a second child cut at her heart even deeper. I encouraged her to spend a few days with me in Chicago because she felt somehow, that there was something more she could have done. She kept blaming herself...

~~

Your sister Sharon, my third daughter, my sixth child, was so sick, sufferin all the time, she was so young. I used to tell her if she didn't change her ways, rippin and runnin and stay home sometimes with her child, it would catch up with her. After she died I used to blame myself, thinkin somehow, I brought it on by prophesizin on her. It worried me for a long time, almost took me away from here. Now I know that it was foolish thinkin. She left her daughter to me and your Daddy to love and care for, and we did. I asked God not to let me live long enough to see another one of my children die. That's the worst hurt a mother could have. (sighs) Silly me, God knows best, he giveth and he taketh away. I know he will give me the courage I need to carry on!

LOVE AND MARRIAGE

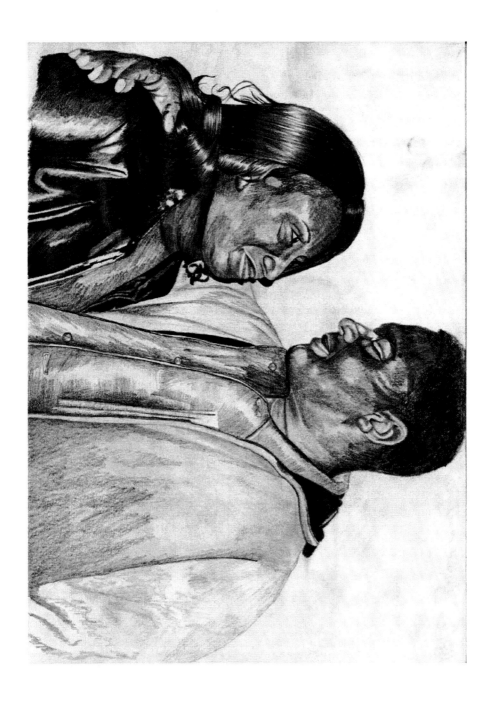

~ ~

Marriage ain't easy, life ain't either. When
I was younger, your Daddy and me might have
separated, but it wasn't just us, we had you
all to think about. So, we stayed together
and made it work. If its enough feelin there
to be saved, then you should try. I guess
that's what the preacher means when he says
'For better or worse'. I am glad we stuck it
out, your Daddy ain't the best, but he sure
ain't the worse, and I ain't either.

~ ~

My cousin Jimmy, got married to the nicest
lady, her name is Ollie. He said he was tired
of the streets, the fast women; wanted
somebody he could trust and would truly care
about him. Like I always told him, ain't
nothin like havin someone you can make a life
with!

~~

Love is more than just hugs and kisses baby, it's stayin in there through the hurt and disappointments of life.

"Love's Quiet Moments"

We lay here free of all thoughts, outside of ourselves. As serenity enfolds us, our bodies are revealing and sincere. Your strong figure is now an extension of mine, with hands gentle, yet firm, that moves with the artistry of a sculpturer, down and around, touching and caressing the center of my being. Our lips are hot and searching, melting into one. Enjoy, this is love's quiet moment!

Our throbbing pulse playing a melody of tranquillity and splendor, creating beautiful music between two hearts beating as one in the night. Our eyes form a mirror for each to see a place of love, pleasure and contentment. You are mine and I am yours, for this moment, it is forever.

If I can let me live it over and over again, for life is as rich as each and every quiet moment my love, I spend with you.

I remember the occasions when Madear, for one reason or another, was angry with Daddy and during those times she would go about her house chores singing hymns, and saying little or nothing to him and very little to us. You could always tell when there was something on her mind that was troubling her. We would come home and find her sitting at the window starring out, singing one of those sad, haunting, southern hymns. When she was like that everyone knew just to leave her alone. My strong willed father would even become timid and ask me to fix his dinner, lunch and breakfast. Whatever my mother was angry about my father would quickly make sure she was satisfied, especially if he wanted everything to return to normal, and boy, was I glad!

I recall another turning point in my life as a woman, it was after a failed relationship and a baby. I didn't know how to tell Madear, so I kept my pregnancy away from her for as long as I could, even though I was a responsible adult. For a while I felt I had let my family down being an unwed mother; they had looked up to me and the dreams I always talked about, but I was wrong. My daughter brought joy and love into their lives as she did mine. Madear never gave up on me, and suggested I not give up on my dreams. 'God gives you no more than you can bear', she often said. She was never too far behind when we needed her for that extra boost whether we welcomed it or not.

As a child I never thought much about it, but looking back as a woman now, I realize there were times my mother felt tied down, hampered from growth. Living with a man like my father, who believed like his father that a woman was meant just to do her husband's bidding, washing, cleaning, cooking, taking care of the children and him, but nothing for herself. There was a time when it was slow at the plant where Daddy worked, Madear took a part-time job at a restaurant; I remember they quarreled and he made her quit after the first weekend. He felt it took her attention away from him and us. I think she wanted to get out of the house, get a breather, maybe discover another side of herself. After the youngest, Denise, was in high school she started going to bingo, traveling and socializing with her alumni, as well as more church activities. Even later getting a job with the Urban League, working with their food kitchen for the needy. Somehow, I guess, after ten children, she gained the strength and self confidence to say to Daddy, 'I am going to live a little now, you can join me or stay at home,' something he had grown comfortable with. He grumbled many times, but realizing it was now a loosing battle, he often joined her.

~ ~

Your Daddy got mad 'cause I kept on braggin 'bout you writin for this newspaper in Chicago, and how you was able to get us a picture with B.B. King. I showed that picture to everybody, put it right on the wall next to the television. One day, I came home from bingo, me and your Daddy got into a big fight about that picture. He snatched it off the wall and tore it up in little pieces, said he didn't want that man's picture on his wall. I was so mad, I couldn't believe it, a grown man, jealous over a picture. I guess after all these kids, and all these years, I still got his interest! (smile)

IT AIN'T MY BUSINESS BUT...
Unsolicited advice from a mother

~ ~

You've got a free trip to Los Angeles to visit your sister Deborah, and even Vegas for a couple of days, if you go with me by train. I know it will be a long ride, but the scenery is beautiful, and you know I ain't goin by plane. Besides it will give us a chance to spend a little time together.

That trip to Vegas was one of the most exciting and fun filled events that I ever shared with my mother. It made the long tiring trip by train from Detroit to Los Angeles and then the bus ride from Los Angeles to Vegas worthwhile. But the combination of the traveling and the Vegas heat, caused me to take ill the first few hours after reaching Vegas, and sent me in and out of the bathroom. My sister Debra, Madear and I were like children in a candy store, racing around from machine to machine. Madear actually put money into a machine and it went off with flashing lights and all. She was confused because no money came down, she thought she had broken it. She raced off searching for us, by the time we scrambled back to the machine someone had claimed it and won, only God knows how much. The last day of that Vegas weekend, Debra and I were reduced down to the penny machines. But Madear, even though she had won, then lost on a variety of games, namely poker that she had learned to master by playing with a little club group back in Detroit, with her motherwit had kept enough money to feed her grown and very grateful daughters.

Our mothers love for us was special, but not unique. Maternal love is universal, as stated so clearly by novelist, Florida Scott-Maxwell, a mother and a woman who accomplished great heights, well into her nineties. 'A mother's love for her children, even her inability to let them be, is because she is under a painful law that the lives that passed through her must be brought to fruition. It is not easy to give closeness and freedom.' (Penguin Books, 1979 'The Measure of My Days')

Experiences with my mother and family enabled me to realize that parenting is an unspoken agreement of love, guidance and dependability given by the adult in return for respect and honor from the child.

"HOME"

Home was....
*a front porch Granny, sitting, waving, and smiling, wisdom eager
to impart*

*the succulent aroma of a delicious hot home-cooked meal, seeping
through an open window*

*a bright shining kitchen, Mom humming a peaceful light-hearted
tune*

*it was the coming together of family, sharing warm conversation,
laughter, happiness and love on quiet caring evenings, with
unlocked doors to neighbors, no visit was too soon.*

Home is....
*an empty face child with keys hanging loosely around its' neck,
entering a dark, curtain drawn room, no hugs or kisses will he
get thawed out, store bought dinner for a late evening bite. Doors
and windows gated, old and young are out of sight*

*the irritable remarks of parents to each other and to their
children as they sat, with mute expressions around a television set*

*a single, lonely mother tired and drawn from life's bitter plight,
strikes out at her children as in spite.*

Home, Sweet Home, *we struggle to remember, but we are
destined to forget. The simple values of life has disappeared, a
loss we are living to regret.*

~~

Child you got to be an example for your children, you can't be layin' round with any man in front of them if it ain't their Daddy.

~ ~

Can't get no more out of a child than you put into them, that's the same thing with a marriage.

~ ~

You don't slap children round their heads. I
don't care if they is yours. You don't whip
no child that way, you could hurt them. Plus,
you make them grow up mean and angry, and
that's no good, 'cause you gonna keep havin
problems with that child. You give them love,
and when you tell them somethin you stick to
it, so they know you mean it! When they step
out of line, one good look from the corner of
your eye will let them know you ain't playin.
You won't have to do a whole lot of spankin
and yellin either. But, when you do have to
spank them, the few licks you give them will
mean somethin 'cause they'll know you care!

~ ~

You think a decent man gonna take you anywhere in public, cussin like a sailor and lookin like a harlot!

~~

I know it ain't my business but, if a person wants to marry you and you care about them, you better go 'head on and marry them, life ain't forever. You know that livin together stuff don't mean nothin. That's like feedin a cow that don't even belong to you, when its ready to give milk, somebody else done claimed him!

TAKING RESPONSIBILITY

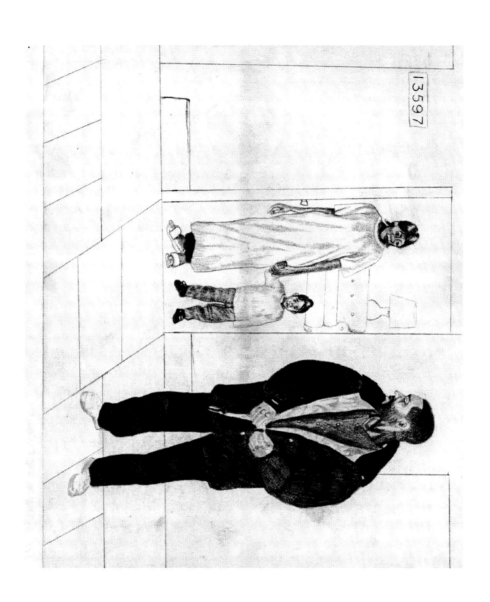

131

~ ~

When you messin with a married man or woman
you headin for a big heartache even if they
care for you, they still ain't yours, and it
ain't right to be in the middle of them and
their mate. Foolin 'round like that don't
work out 'cause they just straddle the track
and you just runnin' 'round carryin a water
pail with a hole in it!

~ ~

When you think you old enough to make your
own decisions, then you old enough to live by
them!

~ ~

Your brother Joe's children, is mad at me,
says I never call 'em. I am the oldest, and I
am they grandmother, if they ever wants me I
am here. Ever since them kid's father died, I
did what I could to reach out and keep them
close to us. Now, they grown and they free to
call and come when they want to. They part of
us, nobody got to prove nothin to the other!

~ ~

Your sister is busy in every organization
with her children. She's done a good job
raisin them all by herself, like you with
your daughter. She just don't have no
personal life since her marriage broke up
some years ago. Now they growin up so fine, I
bet their father wished he was part of their
lives now, but he threw that away. Her
daughter looked so nice on her prom night,
had the prettiest white dress, (smile) looked
like a weddin gown, it sure was grand!

~~

Your baby sister is havin a hard time right
now, why don't you give her a call?   I am
afraid she is gonna worry herself sick about
her   daughter.   These   kids   is   somethin
different, they come in the world thinkin
they know everythin. All she can do is just
leave her to God. Her daughter got so much
talent too, you outta read some of the stuff
she writes.

~ ~

I always told my boys, don't be beatin on no woman, they know that ain't right. They got sisters and daughters, how would they like someone to beat up on them? It don't show love, it don't show they no man either. It shows they a coward that's all.

~~

A real friend won't ask you to do anythin that could get you into trouble. Just remember that, when it's your turn to be somebody's friend!

~ ~

If its honest, you don't have to keep it a secret, you can talk about it. If that makes you a big mouth, then you an honest one!

~ ~

Don't look for blame, its always two sides to everything, the question is what are you gonna do about your side of it?

~ ~

You can't hide the truth, it will find its
way to the light!

~ ~

I told her that she done made her bed, now
she just have to sleep in it. Maybe the next
time she'll make it up with some clean
sheets!

~ ~

Child I told these kids I'd help them all I could, if they're tryin to work or somethin. Other than that, they gonna stay at home and take care of their own babies. Should have thought about rippin and runnin before they had them!

~ ~

These men runnin away from their babies and responsibilities will cause them to miss out on many of life's joys, and pleasures. Like my first time in Vegas. Not knowin any better, I left a flashin machine 'cause I thought I had broke it, and I didn't want to take the blame. But someone else claimed it and got the blessin. Runnin, out of ignorance, or not, can cause you to lose a lot of the good God has for you!

~ ~

That baby brother of yours Gary seems like
he's been here before, always so serious.
Knew what he wanted and went after it. Workin
that good truckin job every day. Now, he is
tight, ain't gonna give out anymore than he
have to, but he is reliable. Him and his wife
pull together; daughter in private school and
his house all paid for. I told them other
sons, ain't no need to be jealous. They could
have the same things if they get their lives
together, and put God in it!

~ ~

After Poppa died, we all took turns takin
care of our baby brother; he was the only boy
out of seven of us. It was rough 'cause he
couldn't find work, and the husbands
complained about takin care of him. Finally
he went off to the war...we never saw him
alive again. My brother never wanted to go,
he just couldn't do nothin else. Like I
always tell you children, put somethin in
your head to hold on to...God bless the child
that got his own!

PRIDE and SELF CONFIDENCE

149

~ ~

I keep tellin that gal, don't let no man make
no fool out of you. You can do that good
enough on your own!

~ ~

You wouldn't even know your brother now. He's stopped drinkin, and he's gettin his weight back, lookin for work and everythin. He looks real good now, God sure did answer my prayers....But, I got to keep on prayin for your brother in California, all hooked up in those drugs. Pray the devil will turn him a loose, and he can get his life back together again. I don't know how he strayed so far away!

It's as though Madear is still praying because our brother in California is now working at becoming independently stable and drug free.

~ ~

Charlene's daughter remind me so much of her when she was alive. Can do anything with a head of hair, but I worry about her 'cause she don't seem to know what she wants to do. And you can't hardly tell her nothin 'cause she's so sensitive. I told her the world ain't gonna care about her feelings. She just gotta be steadfast and keep faith, God will show her the way. It won't be easy, but nothin worthwhile is.

~ ~

I keep tellin my children, you don't use or abuse people. Don't matter if they relatives or not, if you burn the bridges that bring you across, then you never be able to cross them bridges again!

AGING and FEAR

155

Being from a large family, you appreciate so dearly a bed of your own and spending quiet hours alone in solitude. However, returning home to family always held its own special enchantment

~ ~

Hi Sweetie, still comin home for Thanksgivin? Your Daddy done bought a big turkey, and I am gonna start preparin my dinner a little bit every day. Then save my cakes and pies for last. Sure gonna be good to have all my children home again!

~ ~

You should try to come to the family reunion
this year, get a chance to see people you
ain't seen in a long time, and some you ain't
never seen. It shows you where you come from!

~ ~

I am sittin here just lookin at your daddy Joe, grinnin and tearin open these Christmas gifts and just holdin on to those house shoes you bought him. Says they the main things he needed. And all those pretty things y'all got me, I get so happy with my children, I could just burst wide open. Your sister called in from California this mornin too.

~ ~

I don't know why people worry so much about
their age, they blessed to be here. A lot of
folks didn't make it. Your Daddy always say,
only way to stop gettin older is to die. You
can't have it both ways!

~~

The only serious problem I have with agin is that your body jumps way ahead of your spirit. You end up with the will of a thirty year old, locked in the body of an achin seventy year old!

~ ~

That fishin rod and all that other stuff your
Daddy got from the retirement party you kids
gave him, is still sittin here. That man
ain't goin nowhere away from this television,
hangin around botherin me all day. He says he
ain't never had a chance to rest since he was
a little boy. Now that he is free from the
automobile factory, he is gonna do only what
he wants, and I guess that's nothin!

~ ~

After the house got broken into, while at your brother James' second weddin celebration; your Daddy said, he ain't goin to another weddin where these kids keep gettin married two and three times. He said you suppose to get somebody you want to be with and stay with them like he did.

~ ~

I got me a part-time job, workin with the
food pantry at the Urban League. Don't worry
about me, I feel good, it's an easy job. I'll
have my own money, and I can have a break
from your Daddy, fussin like an old woman all
the time. The older he gets, the grumpier he
gets!

~ ~

Your third brother James, you know he has a fit when you call him by his childhood nick-name, 'Bumpty' now. He had all those old women at my alumni dance in Canada, grinnin and pullin over him. He danced with all of 'em. We really had a lot of fun! Now he can charm the ladies, I guess that's why his wife Diane is so crazy about him. That's one son that will come by the house, give me money for bingo, and sit around with his Daddy. Even though he gets on my nerves sometimes, comin in from outside puttin his fingers in my pots. Got the prettiest daughter, but they know they done spoiled her. I jus wish he took life a little more serious!

My mother, elegant! In her cream lace dress, beamed like a young bride as she stood in the chapel entrance of her church. With her original maid of honor, she prepared to renew her wedding vows, after fifty years of sharing life with Daddy. It was a big event for us too, because we were able to express our love and gratitude for all they had been to us. We made it a joyous and memorable occasion. The reception resembled that of a homecoming reunion, with relatives, and everyone we had grown up with, along with new friends.

Daddy smiled and danced with Madear around the floor, looking quite stunning in his cream tuxedo; it was barely noticeable that he had suffered a mild stroke a few years back. He always had a flair for clothes, but he never took anything seriously; like why he couldn't wear a regular tie versus the bow tie that came with his tux. Birthdays, holidays, whatever, he never could understand the fuss. He would always say, 'your mother wants to do this', or 'I don't care, do it'. Now, don't get me wrong, Daddy was not a 'yes' man. If there was something you were trying to pin him down to doing that would bring money out of his pocket, he would buck like   a   bull!

~~

You children sure did it up for me and your Daddy. People still talkin about how nice our fiftieth anniversary was. Your Daddy made me so mad that mornin, fussin over wearin a bow tie I started not to walk down the isle with him again. (smile) Y'all made me so proud, I felt just like a young girl again, and your Daddy looked so handsome. If I die today or tomorrow, I couldn't be happier!

"Here We Stand"

Like the sun beaming down it's hot rays in the early noon
of a mid-summer's day, our love soared with wings of
passion, great expectation, we were giddy like children at
play.

Down a strange, new path we walked together, our lives
now intertwined. Our hands reached out to grasp all the
fruits of life and joy that we both could find.

Through us and around us life blossomed, like a beautiful
bouquet of roses. Through the years the ill winds that blew
caused the stems to bend, some petal weakened and fell
away. The tears, like rain came, nurtured our garden and
made it stronger for another day.

Good or bad we have gladly shared all that one person
could share with another, so now we grow mellow, like fine
wine, with the passing years of time, in our world of loving.

It is often wondered if one had to do certain things over
again, would they? Well my dearest, as the world stands in
witness, here we stand now to reaffirm our devotions.

Our lives full of treasures, rich with love and of living. We
thank God that we met and for all the pleasures he has
given.

Written for Madear and Daddy's 50th Anniversary

~ ~

That man at the corner store was sayin what a handsome couple Mia and Paul make. Everybody loved them weddin invitations, him in his Marine uniform and my granddaughter lookin pretty just like a doll. I always knew they would get together, and I'm prayin to God that they don't let this world pull them apart. We're proud of you too, Baby. You done a good job raisin Mia without a father. My! My! I got grown grandchildren now! Time do fly!

~ ~

Your Daddy and me doin okay, the doctor say,
his sugar is under control, but he still eats
a lot of junk he ain't suppose to. I got a
few aches and pains, guess it's part of
gettin older. I am tryin my best to keep my
pressure down, got enough pills here. Try to
take care of your body baby, there's nothin
like being healthy!

A blinding headache was one of the serious signs of illness for Madear, that I can remember as a child. An ambulance, sirens blaring, took Madear to the hospital. She had been lying down all day, and we were told to be quiet, since the slightest noise aggravated her pain. That was the first time I can recall feeling real fear. Luckily the doctors found nothing wrong, other than stress and tension. They cautioned her to get more rest, and gave her some pills. We were so happy to see Daddy bringing her back home.

She never experienced such a headache again, but some time later she was diagnosed with hypertension, for which she took medicine for the rest of her life.

Madear never allowed any health problems to stand in her way. When my daughter, Mia graduated from high school, she insisted on coming to the ceremony, only to end up in the hospital with one of many side effects related to high blood pressure, and medication.

However, when Mia completed college, she was sitting in the auditorium proud, and spirited, stronger than any ailment.

"As Time Moves On"

'Stop the clock', the woman cried within, 'Stop the clock right now' It isn't fair, this game you play, as you laugh at me from every corner of each passing day.'

'Stop the clock without delay, your starting time was much too fast, you took advantage of my youth, which were wasteful years, the foolish dreams, the hollow laughter, and the empty tears.'

'I am wiser now, I understand, the path is bright and clear, but my legs move slower and my mind is growing nil. I need the time, the strength and swiftness of a child to continue this hard long climb of many, many miles!'

'Stop the time and turn it back, you're ticking much too fast. I've just begun living my dreams of the past, so stop the clock I say, before the sunset of my days.'

The hands of the old father clock continued on, like the sand mills flowing from a glass. The woman gazed into the mirror on the wall, her reflection stared back and with a sigh, she knew then that so many precious moments had already passed her by.

No, old father time wouldn't give in, not even when the aging woman struggled with despair to follow the parade of life going by, full of movement and gaiety in the air.

VIOLENCE and CRIME

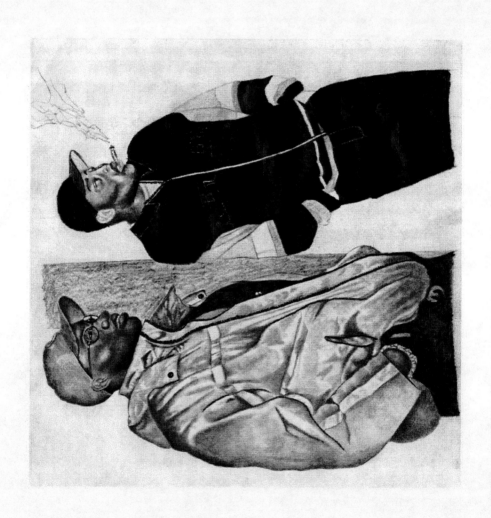

~ ~

These parents today, they ask the child's advice on how to raise them, that's what's wrong. The child is lookin to them for guidance. They're the grown person, they suppose to be raisin the child, the child ain't supposed to be raisin himself!

~ ~

One of your sister's sons got shot in the stomach last night. The doctor said he was blessed, he's gonna make it. I just don't know what's gonna become of these young people today. They're killin off their own generation!

~ ~

I tell my grandchildren, when in doubt, stop and listen to that soft voice deep inside, it's your first mind. That's God talkin to you. Follow it and you won't go wrong.

~ ~

Remember the break-in I told you 'bout, well
your Daddy done went and put up a big red
siren at the top of the house. The whole
neighborhood can see it. He said that's what
he wants them to do. We had the house wired
with an alarm too. You can't open the windows
but so far, or it will go off. The first time
it got real hot, your Daddy snatched open a
window without thinkin; that siren went off
like some fire engine. Dogs barkin, lights
flashin, and we like some fools tryin to
figure out how they said to cut it off. It
sure ain't like it used to be, now everyone
is a prisoner in their own home. I fear for
y'all in this world today!

~~

Kids see so much temptation in the world today. No matter how hard you work with them some gonna go astray, but with the help of God we just gotta keep on tryin to help them find their way.

~ ~

Alright Sweetie, I'll talk to you soon. Take
God with you, you hear? 'Cause these fools
know they done gone crazy. Ain't no place for
nobody, let alone old people like me and your
Daddy, today!

"Baby Boy"
(A Neighbor Sees)

I knew you Baby Boy, when you were so tiny and sweet, curled up warm in your mother's arms so fast asleep, No cares, no fears with the rhythm of her heartbeat you were in a land with peaceful sheep.

I chuckled at you once cheerful boy, retrieving your fallen ball from over my picket fence, with a warm smile, big brown eyes and bouncing feet. Such a playful child full of fun and games with laughter loud, excitement too hard to keep.

I remember clearly as your voice grew husky and your body slim and tall. Girls would snicker and blush each time their name you would call. With a mannish smile you would tease, pulling curls, then talking low, deliberate to please.

I said a prayer for you misguided youth, rushing to be grown it seemed. Hiding in dark corridors with others that had seedy schemes. With your father long gone your mother cries and lose much sleep, as you walk in the shadows of the troubled streets.

I held you Baby Boy when you were so small and meek. Now I carefully lock my doors, afraid to venture out onto the street. The babies I watched grow up and play, now with a gun in hand people dodge and move out of the way.

What happened to many of the Baby Boys we once knew? They're strangers to us now. Manhood some will not see, their dreams, no chance to be. The hope their forefathers gave, now decaying to dust in early musty graves.

From their mother's womb, they were once so tiny and so sweet, now too soon with mournful cries, they're laid to rest so young so cold, forever fast asleep!

ILLINESS AND CONFRONTING THE DEATH OF A PARENT

~~

I keep feelin this hot acid after I eat, doctor want to check it out. He says it probably gallstones. Now don't you go worryin, I'll be alright!

~~

You all don't have to hide it from me, I know
I got cancer, pancreas cancer. They say they
got it all, I'll just leave it in the hands
of the Lord!

~ ~

Don't bring me any more health drinks, I know
you kids are concerned, but you all got my
stomach actin up just as bad, runnin to the
bathroom every five minutes.

~~

I want to eat, God knows I want to eat, but
it makes my stomach cramp so bad. I just have
no appetite.

~ ~

Sometimes I am in such pain, my stomach swells so much that it feels like it's gonna burst wide open. I try not to complain so much. I go up to my room, so your Daddy won't see me hurtin. He comes up right behind me and sits by my bed and just watch me. Every time I frown he ask me what's the matter. He look so scared. We been together so long...I feel sorry for him!

~~

They brought me back to the hospital. I don't know when I am goin home, the doctors still runnin tests. It's better I am here so your Daddy can get some rest, and maybe they can take away the pain!

~ ~

You kids say I am not tryin, but I am, God knows I am. I know if I don't eat, I can't live. One way or the other it will be God's will. I don't want you all to worry about me, I made my peace. I am not afraid of dyin!

Somehow she mustered enough energy to come to Daddy's family reunion dinner in August of that year, for the sake of being with all of her children. I performed my Tina Turner interpretation in tribute to her, as she smiled proudly at me. I danced with my Daddy's brother, uncle Mose, who has since left us. Because of Madear's drastic loss of weight, she lost her wedding rings that night. I guess that was in a way an omen, because that was the last social event my mother attended.

Just before her final bout with her illness, Madear was very concerned about my daughter Mia and her baby J.P., during their return trip home to Okinawa, Japan. The stressful layovers of the military flight caused the baby to contract a high fever and a respiratory infection. Mia's mother-in-law Johnnie and I were worried senseless, as she kept in touch with us both by phone from every stop. I tried to keep it from Madear, but mothers always have this uncanny way of sensing when there is a problem with one of their own.

Madear immediately contacted my sister Deborah, after calling me, and had her book Mia and J.P. on a commercial flight that took them straight into Japan. She said the love Deborah showed was what she wanted us to always have for each other.

~ ~

I know you was worried sick about your child,
being a mother ain't easy, but since you are,
you'd better have a strong heart, 'cause it's
one of the hardest jobs you'll ever have,
especially in these times. It's one you'll
have until the last breath leaves your body.
Your Daddy and me raised five boys and five
girls, and it brought us a lot of joy and
pleasure, that made it all worthwhile.

We talked often after that, but the most
recent call a few weeks later was different,
I didn't know it, but she did.

~ ~

How you doing, Sweetie, do you think you will
be comin home again anytime soon?

I reminded her I was coming for Thanksgiving and inquired if everything was alright. She assured me it was and then she said, **'Take care yourself Sweetie, you hear me?'**. That was the last time I would ever hear her loving, nurturing voice, that I'd taken for granted all those years. The next call a few days later was from my sister Sandra.

James met me at the train station and attempted to prepare me for what lay ahead.

Rushing straight to the hospital into her room, my whole body became numb. The life support system, the monitoring machines, and then my once strong, vibrant mother lying feeble and helpless amidst it all. She was to be connected to it for every moment of life she had left! Everything I did, saw, or said from that point on was like being in a dream. I somehow detached myself from it so that I could survive through it.

This woman, who had been with me my whole life, long before I knew who I was, was about to leave me. Abandonment is the first reaction when someone we love is gone. She saw me, her eyes gleaming damp with tears, and reached out her only free hand, to me. She had made Sandra promise to have the doctors do whatever they could to keep her alive to see all of her children once again.

I found a voice from somewhere to comfort her as best I could, while my heart was breaking, assuring her that we would stick together as a family, keeping her legacy of love alive. I told her Deborah and Rodney were on their way. She appeared more at ease as she gestured for a pad, fighting the effects of the drugs. She scribbled a note, 'Go get somethin to eat, then come back!' In her final hours, she still worried about us. That was her last form of communication, her free hand was soon bound to hinder her from pulling at the tubes that kept her alive.

Deborah was now at her side, with pictures, hoping to arouse a response, a smile, anything. But Madear could only lie there, eyes drifting from side to side like a lost kitten, pausing briefly when Deborah called out to her, focusing in a sad hopeless stare, with words of love and farewell locked forever behind her tearstained eyes. Deborah was devastated!

The next couple of days, suspended between life and death, Madear would go in and out of consciousness. James and Tommy were shrouded in fear and anger. Gary's emotions were suppressed behind a cloak of pride and indignation; Sandra and Denise seemed to be in a daze as they rambled on in aimless conversation. Family and scores of friends filed by her bedside, crying, touching, kissing, and capturing the final moments of her life.

A shrill, long howl from the family dog, on a gray, overcast morning, signaled her farewell.

'*Love opens double gates on suffering. The pain of losing good is the measure of its goodness.*'

Florida Scott-Maxwell

The funeral, on a sunny, crisp fall day greeted, hundreds of mourners. For each of them, as with us, she had touched their lives. I clutched my father's hand as he stood beside me, beaten, motionless, a person that had lost his best friend, his life's companion. My heart went out to my brother, Rodney, a few feet away, who had arrived in Detroit hours after Madear died. His body slumped, sobbing, full of hurt and guilt at not being able to say good-bye. There was sadness for the loss of that gentle lady, with her quick smile, her laughing eyes and her warm loving presence. But, there was also joy and pride to know that she was loved, respected and admired by so many.

The over eighty odd car funeral procession, led by several police escorts, courtesy of the Detroit police department where our brother, James, serves as a volunteer, passed through the old familiar neighborhood, by my parent's home, where the favorite chair of Madear still rested on the porch in the same exact spot.

Closing my eyes I could see her sitting there waving and smiling, as she often did on bright sunny days.

As we laid her remains to rest in Detroit Memorial Park, I knew my mother was finally at peace. Her kind spirit and gracious manner would not lie in a cold grave, but forever lie warmly in the hearts of all who knew and loved her and thought of her as... **Simply Madear!**

My father sad and broken, for awhile resided at home, under the loving care of Sandra, who had proven to be the strongest of us all in spirit and endurance, very much like my mother. I'd like to think that all of her daughters inherited a bit of her strong spirit, inner strength and self confidence and realize that we shared a bond befitting a mother with her daughters.

Daddy was never able to recover from the loss of Madear. In the late winter of '98 the effects of diabetes, coupled with a broken heart, finally took its toll. He left this life that held no more pleasure for him. His death marked a closure in all our lives, in that, we felt they were together again.

After Daddy's funeral Tommy drove me through our old neighborhood, on Scott Street, where we lived and played as children and Brewster Projects, both now industrial areas; Russell Elementary School where Martha Reeves and I shared homework and lasting memories; Northeastern High. All these places are now vacant lots. The Roma Cafe still stands but its glitter and glamour are just fragments of yesteryear where I am now freely allowed to enter. The Eastern Market still exists but it seems so small now.

What is left are memories of my parents; their 50th Golden Anniversary plate proudly displayed on my etagere, surrounded by other articles they treasured; Madear's rhinestone necklace, Daddy's gold and multi-stoned wristband, his twenty years service pin from the auto plant, (Gary kept his thirty year pin). A small 50th anniversary portrait of Madear and Daddy rests beside it. Even though those items are only remnants from their life's journey, they will always be precious to me.

The childhood I remember exists now only in the minds and hearts of those of us who lived through it.

Looking around at my remaining family, we are like branches on a tree, our lives, even though connected, have grown apart in different ways. Each, striving to survive the harshness of the wind. To what extent we have learned and embraced the teaching of caring parents, will make the difference in how we each weather any oncoming storm. Their lessons, shining through the darkness will, surely serve as a **_beacon in the fog_**!

"MOTHER"

Whether the road for her still extends or her path no longer curves or bends Mother is more than just a word, or one we give praise or a present to every now and then.

She is a warm fire on cold winter days.... The aroma of sweet apple pie a baking to the humming of an old spiritual hymn while toiling over dinner she is making.

Her eyes, sparkles with love, watching over you, feeling a sense of pride and thankful to God because of you.

She is the nurturing that continues long after her nest is clear, the call late in the night, worrying and asking, 'Is everything alright, my dear?'

Her amazing faith and maternal strength, that seems never to come to an end, follows her young wherever they go, a virtue by which we all depend.

All grown up now, old enough to wipe away my own tears, shadows in the dark no longer has my fears. I now appreciate and rejoice in her splendor, understanding that her cautious acts was only meant to protect, not to offend me.

Now I savor the memories of laughter and good cheer, holidays full with brothers, sisters and Mom and Dad lovingly near. Time moves so fast, sweet moments like these have passed. Take advantage of right now to say, 'I love you so!', to those twinkling eyes and loving smile, for a better friend you will never know.

Madear November 1922 - October 1993

GLOSSARY

BAD   Slang term used during the 50's through the 70's, meaning something superior or exceptional in the case of clothing e.g., (`BAD SUIT`) highly fashionable.

BIG DIPPER   A cluster of stars shaped like a dipper utensil.

BURLAP   Sacking, a coarsely woven canvas of flax, used to ship potatoes etc., in bulk.

EMMETT TILL   A 15 year old black, Chicago boy killed in the 50's, by two white men in Mississippi while on summer vacation for speaking to a white woman.

MADEAR   (Mud-dear) What some black families of southern influence call their mother or grandmother.

MOTOWN SOUND   A particular type of cross-over music by black, male and female artists and groups made popular during the late 50's through the early 80's, which influenced the sound of popular music all over the world.

                   This name was coined after Detroit's large motor industry by its' originator Berry Gordy.

ABOUT THE AUTHOR

Beatrice Watson

Formerly from Detroit, Beatrice attended Roosevelt University and Columbia College in Chicago where she now resides.

Beatrice, a mother of one daughter Mia, has appeared on stage and television, as a performer and as a guest. She has written, produced, and directed several plays for Community Theater. As a public speaker, she is highly concerned about the future of our youth and the images that are projected in the various forms of media. She hopes that her writings can make a difference.

Beatrice Watson is available for speaking engagements, readings and book signings.

This book is an excellent gift for all occasions.

OTHER PROJECTS BY BEATRICE WATSON

Available for production - Commercial / Fundraising

Plays

Until The Morning - *Musical* (Mother and daughter conflict)

Life Through A Looking Glass - (A woman's inner struggle)

From the Depths of Hell - *Musical/Religious Theme*
(A woman sells her soul for money)
(*Formerly the Deal Maker*)

God's Kids - *Children* (Young boy fight to bring harmony to his family)

Song of Nadafa - (An African fable of human bondage)

Love Black Folks Style - **A situation Comedy**

Selected poems on CD and tapes